EXCESS— THE FACTORY

∞

COMMUNE EDITIONS

Red Epic, Joshua Clover
We Are Nothing and So Can You, Jasper Bernes
That Winter the Wolf Came, Juliana Spahr

A Series of Un/Natural/Disasters, Cheena Marie Lo
Still Dirty, David Lau
Maximum Ca'Canny the Sabotage Manuals, Ida Börjel

Blackout, Nanni Balestrini
Transnational Battle Field, ~~Heriberto Yépez~~
Special Subcommittee, Samuel Solomon

Excess — The Factory, Leslie Kaplan
Cruel Fiction, Wendy Trevino
Duppies, David Marriott

Excess — The Factory

LESLIE KAPLAN

TRANSLATED BY JULIE CARR AND JENNIFER PAP

Commune Editions
Oakland, California
communeeditions.com

An imprint of AK Press / AK Press UK
Oakland, California (akpress@akpress.org)
Edinburgh, Scotland (ak@akedin.demon.co.uk)

Thanks to P.O.L. for permissions and assistance in publication.

Commune Editions design by Front Group Design
    (frontgroupdesign.com)
Cover illustration by Amze Emmons

Library of Congress Cataloging-in-Publication Data

Leslie Kaplan
    [Excess—The Factory. English.]
    Excess—The Factory / Leslie Kaplan; translated by Jennifer Pap and Julie Carr
    Originally published as *L'excès-l'usine* (Hachette, 1982)
    ISBN 9781934639245 (pbk.: alk. paper)
    Library of Congress Control Number: 2018935337

Printed on acid-free paper by McNaughton & Gunn, Michigan, U.S.A. The
    paper used in this publication meets the minimum requirements of ANSI/NISO
    z39.48-1992 (R2009)(*Permanence of Paper*).

for G.

TABLE OF CONTENTS

FIRST CIRCLE

The great factory, the universe, the one that breathes for you.
There's no other air but what it pumps, expels.
You are inside.

All space is occupied : all has become waste. The skin, the teeth, the gaze.

You move between formless walls. You encounter people, sandwiches, Coke bottles, tools, paper, screws. You move indefinitely, outside of time. No beginning, no end. Things exist together, all at once.

Inside the factory, you are endlessly doing.

You are inside, in the factory, the universe, the one that breathes for you.

The factory, you go there. Everything's there. You go.
Excess—the factory

A wall in the sun. Extreme tension. Wall, wall, the small grain, brick
on brick, or cement or often white, sickly white or the crack, a little
earth, gray. Wall, mass. At the same time, this sun. Life is, hatred and
light. Life-oven, from before the beginning, whole.

You are taken, you are turned, you are inside.

The wall, the sun. You forget everything.

Most women have a marvelous smile, missing teeth.

You drink a coffee at the coffee machine.

The courtyard, crossing it.

Sitting on a crate.

Tension, oblivion.

You make cables near the window, cables of different colors. You roll them into coils. Light is there, space is soft. You come, go. Corridors, oblivion.

You make cables near the window. Extreme tension. The sky, and the cables, this shit. You are seized, gripped by the cables, the sky. There is nothing else.

All space is occupied : all has become waste. Skin is dead. Teeth bite an apple, a sandwich. You absorb. The gaze sticks to everything like a fly.

You work nine hours, making holes in parts with a machine. You place the part, bring down the lever, take out the part, and raise the lever again. There's paper everywhere.

Time is outside, in things.

The courtyard, crossing it. A factory courtyard's absolute nostalgia.

You walk between formless walls. Sheets of metal, soft and fat. What interest, what interest. This wire on the ground. No one knows the trouble I see. You go looking for something. You absorb everything. You go, you go down. You see others doing. You are alone, in your gestures. You walk, you feel yourself walking. You are inside. You feel each movement, you unfold, you walk.

You eat caramels, your teeth are stuck together.

Before going in, you go to the cafe. You look at yourself in the mirror above the counter. The jukebox always plays *Those were the days, my love, ah yes those were the days.*

Barrels, wires, sheet metal piled up. Some are painted, red, yellow, blue, green. Parts and scraps, barrels, wires and sheet metal. You don't know, you can't know. You look at them passionately. You're rejected.

You wander in places without names, courtyards, corners, warehouses.

You stop, you go to the cafeteria. Then you come back. Teeth bite, the dead meat is swallowed. You don't eat. Where is the taste? You're penetrated by odors. Everything is already chewed up.

Inside the café, there's always that music. Music and dust, and the mirror over the counter. You drink your coffee while the music plays through, and you go. You pay your money and then you go into the factory.

You wear an apron around your body.

You are near the window. You make cables. Of course, you can die.
The open window, the cables. The air moves gently, you float a little.

Often, you look at yourself in a mirror, a pocket mirror, a reflection.
You look at yourself, you look at yourself, the image is always there.

You take your bike at five in the morning, still dark. You arrive. You see
the factory, it's on the other side of the bridge. One would say it's on
the water. You go there. Excess—the factory.

Barrels, wires, sheet metal piled up. Parts and scraps, the factory. The
places are formless, there are many corners. In the courtyard some
earth, some grass, and all that piled up scrap iron.

You take your bike at five in the morning. You leave. The bike is light,
you grip the handlebars, and you go. When you arrive, the factory is
hot. You are very cold.

It's there, entire, parts and scraps. The factory. There's no direction, it turns. And rises and falls to the right and to the left, of sheet metal of brick and of stone and the factory. And sound and noise. No crying out. The factory. Parts and scraps. Nails and nails. Sheet metal, understand? Soft and fat. Smooth and hard. You don't know, you can't know.

There's no image, ever.

In the courtyard, grass around the scrap metal. The grass grows very well, very green. The metal is piled up.

You drink, that's normal. Words open the infinite. God exists, the factory. No history. It is terror.

You don't know how to do anything.

You put together a gearbox.

You circulate between corners. What's a corner? Three lines. The three goes away. Three lines without the three. You are mad.

You eat a sandwich at noon by the Seine. You sit on a bench, feet swinging. The sky moves slowly. Barges pass. You eat the whole sandwich. It's the middle of the day, you go back into the afternoon.

You make parts at a machine for rubber parts. You sit. The smell of rubber. Next to the chair, a big iron basin. The smell of iron. You count all the parts one by one.

You are nourished with truth. There is only that.

You put on an apron every morning. You take it home on Fridays to wash it. Sometimes you forget the apron in the locker room for the weekend.

You talk; that's normal.

The workshop is full of white sheets, they hang, they overflow the tables, lie on the floor. Moving around is difficult. The sheets are very silent. A large mirror at the back of the workshop reflects them.

The boss is in the booth in the middle of the workshop. In the morning you punch in.

You have a name; yes.

All space is occupied. All has become waste. The skin, the teeth, the gaze. You move between formless walls. You move indefinitely, outside of time. In the morning, you punch in.

You read the paper closely, you search.

You have a wallet with photos inside.

At noon you eat in the cafeteria.

You encounter people, sandwiches, Coke bottles, tools, paper, crates, screws.

Women are there. You watch them.

There is no image ever. Nobody shouts.

You wear an apron around your body.

Women are there.

When you arrive at a new factory, you are always very afraid.

SECOND CIRCLE

From the assembly line, you see everything.

Everything enters, everything enters ceaselessly.

Forced innocence. Pain has no profit.

You have your ten-minute break, you go down to the toilet.

The space is long, cylindrical.

You walk inside, you feel a little lighter. Walls, curved walls.

The line is on the left. You move along the aisle, you go toward the end. Immobile, carried forward, you walk.

The aisle is full, cluttered. Piles of crates, boxes. This and that, rectangles. You walk fairly slowly, you move, you move along.

Some tables are set up on the right, you pass by.

You move, you feel your legs. You feel your stockings, light. You wear a tight skirt, wool, and lady's shoes.

You go along the line, walking. Your feet are on the ground.
You look at the colors.

You are in the factory, you go on.
You unfold, you advance.
You move your thoughts a little.

All this space, all around, curved. The factory is vast.

There is no image. You go down into the empty space, the toilets.

You reach the leader of the line.

She's a heavy woman, she has a grey bun.

You pass by, you look at her. You see her shape.

The woman is sitting. Origin. The pieces arrive.

The woman assembles her parts, absorbed.

Thick body, held in. She is sitting in her dress, on a cushion.

The cushion is crocheted. Next to her, you see her basket. Some yarn spilling out, strands, and some big needles.

The silent fat of the body. You are taken. You look at what has been placed there, hidden.

Time is elsewhere : only space exists, infinite, in your mind, and all life now, gathered and full like a dead stone.

You go down the big curved staircase, you go to the basement.

The stalls are bare, cement.
The place is massive, you enter.

The cement is moist, one would say it was mud. Poured cement, you feel it.
Matter is really strong.

The walls are wide, damp.
Sick water on the walls, you don't like it.

Many stalls, side by side, separated. The white sinks stand out. Thick
basement, fresh matter.

The walls are near, rough.

You play a bit with the faucet, for water.

You are there, weak, with no project.

You have brought a little mirror. You take it out of your pocket, it's a little round one.

You look at yourself attentively. You look for your features.

The face is white, the hair pulled back. You don't remember.

A hand holds the mirror, with the face inside. In a sense, the face is always ok.
You don't remember, you know. You see the circles of sleep, when the constructions fall and rise up again, slowly, in silence.

When you go upstairs, you always pass the tall, beautiful, made up woman in the packing department. Colors, odors, blue and red. Enormous full woman, her big beautiful black hair.

She is standing, her legs spread.

You look at her. You see her legs.

Standing, spread, she moves.

She doesn't stop, she hammers. Her movements overflow and shift and shift, further.

You see her big eyes, open.
You pass her, you sense her body, and then you turn back.

At noon, you go to the cafeteria.

You cross the rounded street. The cafeteria is across the way.

Low houses, in a row. You don't like curtains, useless.

The sky is above, brown. Smoke floats, and on the ground, bits of tubing.

Sweet and lean little street, you are in it. There are lots of black women. Aprons.

You enter, you go to your seat. Tables and benches, and waxed tablecloths. The cloth has little squares, all the same, and it smells.

Childhood.

You sit down, you look around. Steaming dishes, stewed fruit. Oranges and bread, and oily salad. Elbows on the table, you look around.

Unbreakable glasses, big and round, the cutlery gray, flimsy. You often put little spoons in your pocket for the house.

You are there, in the bright frame of the cafeteria, sitting, and in your head there is the image, a young woman in the bright frame of the cafeteria, sitting.

THIRD CIRCLE

You stand at the assembly line, it's an assembly line for crackers.
The workshop is next to the oven, it is very hot. You pick up a row of
crackers, you place them into a bag. The line moves on. You fill the
bag. Your fingers are raw from the grain.

The line moves on. The bags are foiled paper. The crackers are very hard.

In the courtyard, before you come in, you already smell the flour.
When you are in the courtyard, you're not in the workshop.

There's a machine to close the bags.

You are standing at the line of crackers.
Workshop next to the oven, it is very hot.
The crackers go by quickly.
You have your head in a scarf.

From the line you see a corner with piled up boards and sheet metal.
You look and look. Boards and sheet metal and the three lines of the
corner. There are also rags.

Under the boards and sheet metal there is cement. The boards and
sheet metal go in all directions.

The rags are weak.

The boards are thicker than the sheet metal.
Sheet metal, smooth. The little lines go in all directions.
The cement is on the ground.
There is oil on the rags.

Infinity is here. You look.
You are on a stool, above the ground, tense.
The line is a little high.

All around, columns of air. Little waves curving.
Endlessly space folds and unfolds.
You are not supported, there is nothing between the lines.

The space folds open. Walls and partitions, corners, cement. Sheet
metal, understand.
Soft and fat. Boards and wood.
Cement and screws. The cement is on the ground.
The little lines go in all directions.
You don't know, you can't know.

You go outside, in the café music is playing.
Images stand out.

You go shopping. The grocery store, it's all the same.

Upstairs, the room waits.

You go there. In a sense, the room is always too big.

You eat without hunger. Where is the taste?
You bite the teeth of the other.

You look at a fingernail, an elbow, an eye.
You look and look.

You are immobile. You circulate between walls of flesh, little blood-
rivers. The body works and falls. You go nowhere, pleasure is hard,
transparent.

You sleep in a nightmare. You slip from room to dream, the substance
is the same.

The room is a room. You pay rent.
You live, you die, each instant.

The suburb, it's all the same. Space, space kills.

You stand at the bus stop. You wait for the bus. Sky and telephone poles all around. The sky is full of wires.

The sky is immense. There are these wires. You wait for the bus. The road is there.

The buildings are erected in the middle of fields. The bus stops in front of some buildings, it doesn't stop in front of others.

At the café, music. It's nothing.

You stand at the bus stop, you look at the buildings, over there. You think of the alleys between buildings.

The alleys are open.

Here and now, there and elsewhere, you wait for the bus. The stop is by the café. You smell the dust. The sky is very blue. The air floats. All these wires.

Road is there.

You are outside. You got off the train, you wait for the bus. The buildings come and go. The air breathes, there is breath. Doors open, doors open everywhere, you pass, you pass.

FOURTH CIRCLE

You go to a factory that makes headlights. It's in a neighborhood just outside the center, a little street. At last you've arrived. The factory is there.

You see it, it's in the courtyard, a cadaver without weight. It's there, it doesn't move. Factory mass. You know it.

You are in front, in the courtyard, you think, you know it.

The factory is very big, in many pieces.

Disarticulated and full, the factory.

It's there, it doesn't move. The air is humid, the factory sweats.

From the metro to the factory a soft black space. You're in it, you walk.

You turn in the soft space, you pass by the young woman.
She's sitting on a chair in front of the door.

The young woman is sitting, she's talking to her dogs. There is a bottle
on the ground, it's not important.

The young woman is there, infinite.

Nothing and nothing. The world opens, the world opens in each place.
You are at the end. Things are. Chair and door, and behind, the buffet.

The buffet is large and brown. You see it through the window.
Heavy and large, the buffet. There's also a table with chairs all around
it. The chairs are all the same.

The young woman is there, infinite.

Things in the room, you see them. Colors stand out.
The buffet is brown, the tablecloth is red, the sofa is green.
The curtains are white. Blue tiles on the floor. Yellow walls, so
many colors.

The bottle is on the ground, it's not important.

The young woman is sitting, in front of the door. She's talking to her
dogs. She is blond, bleached hair. You look at her. She has an apron
that wraps around her body.

She is there, on her chair. Skirt and sweater, and over it, the apron.
The body is underneath. Everything is there, everything.

Her legs hang off the chair. Legs, soft. On her feet are square shoes, a
little heavy.

The chair is in the street. All around, that black space.
The sky passes.
The young woman is there, sitting.

The apron ties behind, you've seen it. The face is marked, empty
traces. Skirt and sweater, and the full forms of the body.
One is pulled, one is pulled very far.

The street is open under the sky of the factory.
Soft open street. The paving stones, all the same.

The entrance gates are very high, splendid.

Weightless carcass, disarticulated and full,
being there, in the courtyard, it is there, the factory.

Parts, scraps and life, the factory.
And brick and tile. And in and out.
And right and left and brick and tile and soft and fat and turn and turn
and life and life and wood and nail and iron and iron and in and out
and turn and noise.

Never a cry. The factory.

Parts scraps and life, the factory, and iron and iron and life and life and
brick and tile and in and out and life and life and nail and nail.

You don't know, you can't know.

The street is a street under the sky of the factory.

You enter the courtyard.

You see the crates. The boards are there, laid out.
Blue plastic tarps at the back.

You enter the courtyard.

In a corner, the staircase. The staircase is iron, fragile.

Above, the line floats.

You go up.

The staircase is fragile. Iron, how wretched.

Your foot is on the step, open sky. The iron is so thin.

You go up. The woman in front wears a raincoat.

You go up. The sexes are separated.

The men stay below.

Across is the machine shop where the presses are. You never go there.

The line is above, floating.

You look at the woman in front. She has a full waist.

You love her, you love her so much.

You go up by the iron stair.
The street is below.

The staircase is fragile. You rest a little on the landings, you see the pillars.

The landings are made of wood. You go up.

There are pillars at every floor.

Above, the line, floating.

You look at the woman in front. You know her raincoat, you know that fabric.

You're in the workshop with the assembly line.
You're sitting down. The line is going to start.
Palpable air, blank memory.
You're there, you're sitting. Stool. Cartons.

The ceiling is very high. There are pillars.
The workshop floats a little. Thick air, high ceiling.
The line moves on, flat, in the middle of the boxes.

The boxes are easy, you make them with your hands.
Your hands are somewhere else. You think. Thought is sticky.
All around, the workshop.
In the thick air, under the high ceiling, you make boxes, you think.

Thought doesn't come out, it stays inside.
Nothing is taken apart. You think.

High ceilings, pillars. You are in the thick air.
Hands are somewhere else, you think a sticky thought.
You look, you think.

From the line, you look.

Your eyes are open. Around your eyes, space.
Space is silent. Holes of noise, holes of noise everywhere.
Open, in the silent and noisy texture of space, the eyes see.

The silence of the crates is terrible. In the body, all this noise.

The eyes are there, they never stop seeing.

Thick and soft air. Hands are on the boxes,
thought moves on the inside.

The cardboard is easy, it folds easily. Nothing is detached, you make.

The body is in space. In the body, the long thought and ceaselessly,
the little noises.
Things are gripped, thickness of the air.

The vaulted arch above, the high arch.

The air is red, it's the workshop. Outside it might rain. The supervisor walks the length of the line. She shows her wide skirt and her gold teeth. Curved walls, rounded. The workshop is there, entire.

FIFTH CIRCLE

Somewhere else, the hotel.

You are outside, under the tense sky. The hotel is standing, unreal and slender. Meager framework.
The rooms are inside.

The rooms, you know them. Little drowned rooms.

You have come out of the metro. Here is the street, the fruits and vegetables. Weightless café window, placed on the sidewalk. You go in.

Outside, the sky descends. A white wheel, a carnival game. You look at the prize dolls, then you return to the violent, limitless space of the hotel.

From the sidewalk, you see the curtains, the little transparent curtains. The sky advances and penetrates the room. The street is there, very present.

You wander the floors, you pass by rooms.
Hallways bifurcate. The walls are full of water, miserable.
You are in the fragile and complicated structure of the hotel.

In the room, very quickly, thought is raw.

The blanket is on the bed. You sit down, you look at the room.
Time stays there, like a box.

Skin exposed, on the blanket. Over there, there's the big white sink,
and behind it, the cardboard walls.

The air is free, detached. The wallpaper goes on and on. On the bed,
stiff linear effort. No success. There's never an interior.

The furniture's not right. You fall asleep without support.

Blank awakening, inhuman. No bearings, the factory. You are
thrown headlong.

The little humpback is in her place, near the radiator.

She knits.

The workshop unfolds, it's an immense place. Some women are sitting, inside.

Day comes.

You've put on the smock. In the pocket, there are coins for the coffee machine. Sometimes you put your hand in the pocket, to feel.

Soon you will go to the toilets.

Near the toilets is a girl at a counter with a timer.
Next to her, a black woman. You once lent her five francs.

Sun and light. You see the little checks of the apron. The air is sharp, you advance to the end of the world. The black woman is very beautiful.

Fragility, tension. You are sitting, all alone.
Things are there, you can think them.

You can think things.

Blank euphoria, deferred birth. Mounting and diffuse movement, urgency.
Pure urgency.

Everything is there, in idea, everything. You are in the light, stuck. The world turns over, transparent surface. Nothing behind the windowpane. You see yourself being, endlessly.

The little humpback is in her place, near the radiator. She is very small and very young. You see her from behind. When she is standing, one of her shoulders just reaches the table. The table is perfectly clean, rectangular and white. Above there is the window with its obscene ledge. The girl is at the table, you see her shoulders, and her little massive back. She makes her pieces, very quickly, with angular gestures.

The skylight lets the light in, and the sun. Sparks. It is hot. You are absorbed, nowhere, floating at the end of the line.

A woman passes by, at the back of the workshop.

Yellow wall, without information.

The girl next to you talks about her night. The Yugoslavian. Once she put on a blond wig, to look like.

The girl talks, you listen to her. Speech comes and goes, fat little words. A tooth is missing from her mouth, in front, the words come through the hole.

You walk with the girl along the edge of the water. The sky is white. Banks, banks of the Seine. You walk together, you talk to each other, while the sky touches the earth, and the water. Benches, a painted snack bar. Over there, in the distance, you see the big mechanical factory, its sheets of metal.

You hold the girl by the arm, you walk. The sky cooks, immobile. One would say milk. In the water, a barge floats. It's moving toward the bridge.

You walk. You have an apron, the girl has a smock. The trees are detached, stiff and green. The sky hovers.

The barge has reached the bridge. The air moves a bit. You look at the little boat, its red and yellow wood. The water is blue, far away.

You move along the humid earth, you talk. The factory is set over there, you see the tubes and the cylinders. Vague water, you look at it. The barge has left, you feel the slowness of the sky.

SIXTH CIRCLE

It's spring. The factory is fat and cold.

You look, outside.

You arrive through the fields, through the countryside.
You pedal in the air, transparent and closed in.

The countryside is yellow and green.

You pass through anonymous trees. The path crunches, fragile.
You ride on sharp crumbling stones, dry pebbles, gravel.

Slight creatures fly against the wide flat sky.

From far away you see it. It's set on the grass, light. The sheet metal is
thin, undulating.

The windows are all open. The air circulates, identical.

You put away the bike. The courtyard is paved with rounded stones.

In the back, scaffolding. The paving stones make a strange surface, calm.

You cross the air. Between the stones, grasses poke through.

Nothing disappears, ever. The air swells, at each instant, with odors.

You advance through the round courtyard. The sky above, naïve. You are afraid, endlessly.

Women arrive in soft blouses. You have eyes, you see their breasts.

Space is divided. It's terrible.
You are not protected.

You come, you go. Cruel and soft spring.
Factory the factory, first memory.

You are in the workshop, outside it's raining.
The rain falls. Sharp absence.

Things are, contrary, unreal, real.

You have an apron and a bike.
You buy some objects, sure.
You want them.

You cross the city, serious.

The streets go very quickly, broad, narrow, broad, narrow.
There are many little colored kiosks, trees, benches.
Dogs wag their tails, agitated.

You walk, surrounded by houses. Often doors open, and you see the
staircases inside. You stop when you see them rising, steep, behind
the door.

In the middle of the city, the river flows, all alone, and things, you
always already know them, surprised.

You get off the bus, you walk.
Up there, the raw sky, blue and white. You go along the fence.
Behind it, there is the empty lot.

You look between the slots, from outside.
The dirt is spread out, spread out, orange.
Everything begins, without creation. Offering.

You are there, behind the fence. You see the scraps.

People circulate, in caps, dragging bags.

There are bits of paper, soft, disgusting, and there's plastic. The plastic
is old, used up. Slab and fragments. Some locks are lying around.

Rust is there, mysterious.

Piled up barrels, shovels and skins. Square crates, simple. You also see
animal stuff.

Hardened rags, in a ball. What testimony.

Doors are ajar, standing. The sky remains fixed.
Mirrors, also, in frames.

Certain forms are enveloped, it's unthinkable. The worst are small
and fat.

The ground changes, in places. Viscous puddles. Also, corners dry
like eyes.

A fire burns, in the middle.
You look through a slot. It's so real.

You live in a trailer in the middle of a field.
The countryside is all around, in a confusion. Vegetables grow, you
can't do anything about it. The field and the sky are the same. Despair.

Outside, you see mounds, furrows. The field is harrowed, full of lines.
You fade.

Disordered and hard sky. A bird runs across it.
You hear a cry, a cry, a cry.

The air is frozen. Things are there, behind.

You have a book, you look at it. You read.
You are in the middle of a brown field, in the curved trailer,
this cylinder.

In the evenings you go eat in a little restaurant. The restaurant is small,
you hear the owner talking. You are sitting across from the other.
Outside, the rails, from time to time, a train.

You drink, you trace lines on the table cloth. You don't deny yourself
anything, you eat. Afterwards, you leave.

The night is weightless, naked. You walk easily, your arms float
alongside your body. You are on the road between the rows of trees.

Night's matter, weightless, disquieting. You glide, you walk on.
On the edge of the road, you see the trees black and firm.

The air breaks, in places, you feel it. Night without substance, you are
in it, endlessly you cross it. The body trembles, diffuse.
You go, you advance.

The hitting starts, there are reasons. The dress is torn with the skin.

The road rises up, wrinkled and soft, you sink into it. All around you see trees, their grey leaves, intangible.

You feel thrown, immense, and old, like every thing.

SEVENTH CIRCLE

You are in a round factory.

Outside, it's difficult. Night, with some trees.
A light bulb turns, peaceful.

You are on a platform, leaning over. You look.
The elevator goes up and down in a vertical corridor.

There are many doors and windows, you saw them while arriving, they
increase the unease.

The factory is big, really defined.

Powerful light, invisible. The ceiling is far.

There are precise walls, hallways.
The air is breathed, imperceptible.
Thought is there.

You are standing, at the bus stop, you wait for the bus.
All around there is the sky and telephone poles.

The sky advances, immobile.
Big wide sky. You see the streaks.

At the café, music, tranquil and absent.
Those were the days, my love, ah yes, those were the days.

Interminable sky, already frayed.
There is no forgetting, ever. You are run through.

When you arrive, a refrigerator in the corner is big and white.
Some wires over there. Things are hanging.

There are appliances, hollow basins, a counter.
The basins are blue and yellow.
You sit down, you have a drink.

Across, the shelves. They are apparent.
You dream, always. The shelves are edged.

The substance of the room is porous.
A silence. You are sitting.

Presence of volume. Curved things. The wall offers, a lot.

A calendar is pinned up, for the days. Repairs and stitches, and always
this room, run through. Wires. You are there.

On the counter, there are objects. The objects are useless, it's terrible.

Volume swelling, colors. Scraps and things, rubber.
The room slides endlessly. You are inside.

It's evening. You have time.

The tranquil space moves in. Things fall, everything.

There are images on the wall, stuck there, flat. The objects are isolated. Anxiety. All around, the tablecloth and the blanket, and the crocheted bedspread. The curtains too, wooly.

Behind the windows, the suburbs broad and spacious. You feel them. You are among your own, and you consider your dear immobility.

The room is there, all around. No one can know, no one.
You have eaten the meal with your mouth. You are sitting in chairs, there are hands and knees.

Something dies, what violence.

Across, the face of the other, closed and supple like a piece of body.

EIGHTH CIRCLE

There are rails in the sky.
The trains pass.

Housing projects, tall and straight.
The parks marked off by trees.
Streets. You walk.

You are on the sidewalk, you go, you walk.

Between the buildings, the air circulates.
It's the present.

Here and there a little house, very little. You could laugh,
you know?

Empty lots, surrounded. You walk.

Unfolding surface of the boulevard, expanse.
You move forward easily, there is room.

The sky is green, unchanging. You are below it.

Long boulevard, wide.
Over there, the arched iron bridge. By the walls you see some poor
animals, creatures.

Shacks, encounters. City fragmented and full.
A bench, volumes of sand.
You pass by. The light is grey, hidden.

The sky hardens in places. Slabs.

The stores are slightly dismantled, demolished inside.
Irregular shop window, slack. The objects that you see inside are
elsewhere, maybe.

The rails, up high, placed like kings.

Boulevard and pebbles. Small grave streets. Some beautiful trees.
Further on the river floats, white, thick. No one on it.

You know nothing of money, it is so small.

Often you go to the Monoprix.

You go in. Colors. The objects are spread out in their boxes, detached.

You pass through the aisles. You touch a little.
You see yourself in the glass, the mirrors.

You try on one thing and another.
Things, you like them for themselves.

You move in the empty light.
All around, lines, distinct forms.

You look. You look at the easy life of objects.

At the hotel.

The room is square, exterior. Smothering cold.
You eat.

There are things and things and things.

You sleep, you dream.

You are in front of the hotel. The woman in charge looks down from
her window when you ring to go in.

You pass between thick dense dreams, columns. You move forward
among heavy houses, close-set, you pass.

A little above, the skies circulate.
You don't see them, you feel them.

Numerous and rapid skies, low skies.

You advance in a boat, through muddy and narrow streets.

There is no water, ever.

It's an absent city, without history. The houses are old. Inside, the
white tiled floors are cracked, very cold.

The houses and the streets are full, encumbered.
Ruins and packages. You pass.

You go, through cardboard, bottles, creams, meats.

You have skins, illnesses.

You see torn off mouths, lost hair, burned bodies.

You see the Yugoslavian woman, the one whose child is in the hospital. You really see her. She shows the picture of the child, with the scar on its forehead.

You sleep among material dreams.
In the morning, you emerge from sleep drawn by the empty awakening of words.

Sometimes you walk in the cemetery.
It's far, beyond the streets.

You go in through a big rounded gateway. The gate is wide, immobile.
You pass beneath the arch.
On the other side, all the trees.

You walk on the moving paths. The air is soft, fluid. Wet slopes, bushes,
and everywhere trees, slender. Leaves hang on the branches like lies.

Bordering the path, marble plaques and little tombs, bothersome.
The inscriptions are weak. You read them. Names, dates, history.
Nothing is well marked. The sky moves, full of water.

Animals play. It's free.

Something is there in the worn out air, transparent.
You don't know, you remember.

You pass through the leaves. The grass can slip, so green. Words have
no meaning. Where, but where, are the dead?

You arrive. The factory is there.

Spread out fragment, detached and alive.
Huge and powerful fragment, free.

Separate and massive, the factory moves.

You look. Full life, facing you. It's there. The forms are made.

You go in.

There are scaffoldings near the ceiling.
The air is filled with grey currents, superficial.

You are below. You look.

You see the constructions, up there, the confusion of long beams,
possible. It's big.

The windows are open, the gaze.
You are absorbed by the interior and exterior light.

You sit, you make things.

Little table, violent and hard. There are instruments.

You make things. The instruments are very small.

You are sitting, dispersed. Limits of the table. You touch its feet, delicate iron.
You are lost.

All around, deployed and hollow, material things.

When you are thirsty, coffee machine.

You move around often, you walk.
Partitions, suspended. You walk around.

The walls are thin, so light.
You come, you go. Matter is heavy. You are in a drifting and
closed fragment.

Windows are open, the air comes in. These light walls, everywhere.
You don't die, ever.

Fragile papered walls. Corners curling and torn. Blood maybe, some
bolts. Empty mass of the factory, the corridors are long and full.

You pass into the light carcass, thin and suspended, of the factory.
You are in matter that expands, fat matter, plastic and stiff.

Behind a pile you see the girl squatting, in pants.
Sweet little girl. She has glasses around her eyes.

She reads, always.

You take corridors, you go. Crates to the side, obstacles. Beautiful
passages, difficult. You go.

Flat roof and surface. Upright tubes, pipes. Some parts of the factory
are in the open air. You go on.

Tucked away corners, piles and stacks. Overturned ledges. Furrows.
Scraps are present, prominent. You also see the remnants of walls.

The other workshops, you don't know them. You think about them.

You see interlocking frames, staircases.
Steps go up and down. The air is suppressed, you see lines above all.

There is an intense activity, singular.
People, as if in frescoes, you cannot pass behind them.

In the hallway you encounter a young French girl. She is an unfinished girl. She pushes a cart.

She stands up straight when you pass. She looks at who you are.

She carries a transparent plastic bag. Inside it is a photograph of her, you see it.

You look at the girl. Her body is not well covered up, she seems naked inside. You see her round head and her stiff hair.

The mouth is open. The space is bound, it holds. You forget.

The workshop grows wide, wide. She cries often, like at church. It's naïve.

You see her, you look at her. Scraps drag. The workshop is full of remnants of her, you don't leave her.

Life descends, vertical. Naked matter. You are inside, it's the strict whirlwind, eternity.

NINTH CIRCLE

It's in a working class quarter, an old square, very beautiful. You drink a coffee at a table under the arcades. The lines of the façade are so simple, so harmonious, and a very old nostalgia grips your heart and the air.

You sit, you drink. All around, the pink stones. The air is light, transparent, almost liquid. Up above, the sky, rigid and blue, like a piece of cardboard.

Music plays. *Those were the days, my love, ah yes those were the days.*

In the middle of the square, a fountain. Matter of the air, sound of the water, weakness, everything dissolves and begins again. You float.

You see the pink stones, cracked and porous. People come and go, slowly, absent. Where are things?
It's the end of the day. You see the lines of the roofs. Firm lines, well drawn. The square is so beautiful. All around, that sugared air.

At the end of the square, there is a big statue, heavy and precise, a king on horseback, as there often is. The square bears his name.

The heat is a little unreal. You are enveloped, and at the same time, everything is far away.

You sit, you watch. The square is old, badly kept. The walls are crumbling, flaking. This time that stretches and turns ceaselessly, as at the origin. Nothing is happening, something is happening, you are outside of time, under the sky of the factory.

At the next table is a group of women. They drink while talking to each other. You watch them.

The women are there, sitting, in their ordinary clothes. They're very made up, with hair of all colors. You watch them. You see the violent makeup around their damaged eyes, around their open gaze.

These are used women.

The women sit around a table, drinking and talking under the old arcades, on straw chairs a bit broken, in this old square, more or less abandoned, or maybe they'll restore it one day, who knows.

Off to the side is a little girl.

The little girl seems ageless, but she is still very young.

She plays with a baby, very gently. She holds the baby on her knees, jiggles it while humming, presses it against her. Then she pretends to drop it. The baby cries. She smacks it, she bites at it, and hugs it again.

The baby is very ugly. Little grey baby.

The girl repeats her game again and again. The baby has skin like rubber.
The little girl bends the baby, squeezes it. At one point the woman
who might be the mother says to the little girl : Come on, you're going
to kill the baby. The little girl lifts up the baby and asks : Do you think
I'm going to kill you?

TRANSLATORS' AFTERWORD

Leslie Kaplan came of age in 1960s Paris. At that time, France was defined by a particular brand of conservatism, even while tumultuous events called out for dramatic response. Lofted by crisis in the Algerian colony, President Charles de Gaulle had successfully pushed for strong executive power when a new constitution was written, founding the Fifth Republic (1958). De Gaulle believed that a united and powerful France could re-emerge from war and post-war challenges through fidelity to traditions and commitment to social stability. Attaching paramount importance to French identity and destiny meant paying little heed to the varied needs of working class people and other vulnerable populations. Within this ideology there was much to concern those committed to social justice.

While De Gaulle would yield to the necessity of decolonization, the French army's practices of torture were revealed in the course of the turbulent Algerian war for independence (1954-62). In her autobiographical *Mon Amérique commence en Pologne*, Kaplan evokes this history by naming one of the victims in a single line: "La torture. Djamila Boupacha" (68). The rape and forced confession of this young Algerian militant was revealed and brought to international attention through the efforts of Simone de Beauvoir and Gisèle Halimi in 1960. Kaplan also remembers violence perpetrated in Paris itself by the OAS (Organisation Armée Secrète), a far right group committed to keeping Algeria French: in 1962, a bomb destined for Culture Minister André Malraux caused the loss of an eye for a four year old girl who lived in the same building. There was, of course, the Vietnam War, which galvanized the French population as it did the American. These events and others on the domestic front generated a growing sense of outrage for many on the left and mobilized an entire generation, of which Kaplan was a part, toward political awareness and activism.

At age 21, with the desire to redress inequalities, Kaplan traveled to newly liberated Algeria to teach French; back in Paris, she taught courses to workers who had little or no access to the French university system. Soon after, as a university student of philosophy and history, she joined the radical student group, the Union of Marxist-Leninist Communist Youth (UCJML), which had split from the French Communist Party. The UCJML had its own list of principles, including its adaptation of Mao's notion that it was essential for revolutionary intellectuals to work alongside the proletariat. Kaplan and others who called themselves "établis" took jobs in factories with the intention of identifying and joining radicalized workers in revolution.[1] The protest movements of May 1968 would soon gather force, particularly at the Nanterre campus. Soon after, a general strike broke out throughout France involving about nine million workers, almost half the working population, with an energy that seemed to the activists to mark the beginning of a new order, a new France at least, liberated into communism. Kaplan describes the work stoppage at the Brandt factory in Lyon where she worked at the time, and the extraordinary transformation of the space, now occupied by workers. Now they were individuals speaking to one another:

> People invite each other to come see their work spaces. Until then, it was not allowed to go into another work area besides your own. For the first time, workers circulate in their factory, which seems extraordinary: the factory belongs to us. Above all, you have the feeling of time. The time to talk to each other, to know each other. I had never spoken with the women who worked with the heavy presses, who worked on big machines; really big women who went all out with their makeup and their femininity. Time becomes a way to meet, and also to imagine.[2]

The hopefulness was short-lived, however. De Gaulle's government, abetted by the leading labor unions, enforced a return to the usual order. Despite this crushing disappointment, Kaplan went back to the factory in the fall of '68, remaining for another two years, feeling that there was still something to be learned there.

Ten years after these transformative events, Kaplan began *L'excès-l'usine*, her first book. Its publication by Hachette in 1982 was noticed immediately and sparked a variety of strong responses, including an extensive interview with Marguerite Duras, and a review by Maurice Blanchot in *Libération*. Television appearances, radio interviews, and reviews of the book in literary journals across France followed. For some at the time the book seemed to offer no hope for the worker, no agency that could free her from the abject alienation of the assembly line. This line of thought continues to echo as when, in 2005, Slavoj Žižek writes, "*L'excès-l'usine*, with its description of the 'Hell' of the factory life, renders palpable the dimension overlooked in the standard Marxist depictions of the workers' 'alienation.'" For Žižek, the power of the book lies in its ability to conjure the factory as a place void of memory and hope, where workers "lose the very capacity to dream, to devise projects of alternate reality."[3] And yet, this interpretation doesn't fully allow for the peculiar complexity of the book, which, even with its sometimes bleak focus on corners, cement, wires, and hallways, also notices the isolated traces of human lives.

In writing *L'excès-l'usine*, Kaplan was wary of using an overproduced or too-familiar language to convey the workers' experience of capitalist production. The usual discursive practices would only pervert, not reveal, her subject. A stripped-down language was needed, freed from the forms and expectations of discourse. Rather than being descriptive or explanatory, the poem's language would be "suspended," with objects and events seemingly set loose from their context. As she writes:

> No discourse can say the factory. One needs suspended and discordant words. Open words. You can't dispense with the factory with words, and the words that write it have to take that, their own limit, into account.[4]

Faced with the desire, or with the ethical summons, to write about an alienating and often hidden place in society, Kaplan wrote *L'excès-l'usine* with a new strangeness that acknowledges the distances that factory environments generate between people and between people and objects. Kaplan's poetic voice circulates through the factory with its heaps of wire, sheet metal, its assembly line rhythms, and its open yards. As such, she renders into poetry what is political life—the position of the workers in the factory and their isolation from the value they are producing.

One of the striking aspects of *L'excès-l'usine* is the choice of the third-person pronoun "on" to designate the subjective presence that moves through the book. "On" has more than one English equivalent: "one," a vernacular "we," or the generalized "you," depending on context. "One" tempted us as translators because of its refusal (like the French "on") to designate a specific individual, but in the end it sounded too elevated for this work. "We" suggests a coherent community that clearly does not exist in these poems, which convey the isolation of each rather than the belonging together of many. Thus, we have translated "on" as "you," which in English has the advantage of sometimes referring to the self, sometimes to a specific other, and sometimes to anybody. "You," then, offers the floating subjectivities of this assemblage of persons made disconnected by the factory system.

The refusal of coherent subjectivity leads Maurice Blanchot to write of *L'excès-l'usine* in 1987 that: "(t)he 'On' is the mark of an 'I'—a subject without 'subject'—that has renounced singularity without achieving anything in common" (131-2). Furthermore, Blanchot saw in Kaplan's poem the endless repetition inherent in not just the factory, but in the human condition more broadly: "Vous n'en sortez jamais."

> Other remarkable books have described the work done by a factory and in a factory. But here from the very first words we understand that, if we enter into working in the factory, we will belong henceforth to the immensity of the universe ("the great factory universe"), there will no longer be any other world, there has never been any other: time is finished, succession is abolished, and "things exist together, simultaneously." There is no more outside—you think you're getting out? You're not getting out.[5]

Marguerite Duras also singled out the book for its ability to capture the isolation and emptiness of factory life: "this piecemeal activity, minuscule, always identical to itself, that destroys the individual, kills the individual in her very spirit [*génie*]."[6] In their extended 1982 interview, Kaplan and Duras discussed these aspects of

the book, going so far as to suggest a parallel with Robert Antelme's depiction of the concentration camps in his *The Human Race* (1947).

However, despite the bleak landscape of labor and loneliness that indeed dominates these poems, there are moments of connection and tenderness that seem to us to offer, if not a "way out," at least an alternative reality hovering in the margins. We find examples of such tenderness in the way the gaze lingers gently and unobtrusively on women's bodies and faces: "When you go upstairs, you always pass the tall, beautiful, made up woman in the packing department. Colors, odors, blue and red. Enormous full woman, her big beautiful black hair." "Most women have a marvelous smile, missing teeth." These are moments when women's vulnerabilities, their beauty, are made available to the reader. Within the overriding quality of disconnection surprising flashes of connection, even love for the other, emerge: "You see her, you look at her. Scraps drag. The workshop is full of remnants of her, you don't leave her."

And even beyond the silence of looking, there is sometimes speech. "The girl talks, you listen to her. Speech comes and goes, fat little words. A tooth is missing from her mouth, in front, the words come through the hole." "The sky is white. Banks, banks of the Seine. You walk together, you talk to each other, while the sky touches the earth, and the water." These conversations, hinted at here and there, suggest the possibility of further communion.

But the reader must decide what to make of the possibility of speech. The book closes with troubling words spoken between a woman "who might be the mother" and a girl who might be her daughter. Their dialogue suggests that speech is complicit with the continuing violence of the factory. And so we have to ask, do words lose significance in the factory space? Do they blend into a white sky and horizon, heavy with monotony and emptiness? Or might speech sometimes be offered as an answer to this very monotony? The question is open.

In the years since *L'excès-l'usine*, Kaplan has gone on to critique the used-up language of commercial society, and has offered literature as an alternative. Her 2003 book *Les Outils* (Tools) reflects on her own practice and the ways that literature, standing perhaps outside of the language of capital, can carry out ethical projects. She writes of reading as a way to "think with a work: with an object both finite and infinite, made by a person or by many, and which, put into circulation," may become a "tool" to help restore humanity.[7] In a 2014 interview with us, Kaplan developed this more hopeful way of thinking about language:

> Is speech a way of talking to another as though the conversation is already finished? Or…infinite, it would go on forever, because we are alive and we can be born all the time.[8]

L'excès-l'usine makes suffering and alienation palpable. But as poetry, perhaps it also performs the liberating gesture that Kafka claims for writing. As Kaplan notes:

> This sentence of Kafka's has always seemed to me to be the very definition of what writing is: "To write is to jump outside the line of the assassins": the assassins, contrary to what one might believe, are those who stay in line, who follow the usual way of things, who repeat and start over again the bad life as it goes. ("Writing moves the sky")

Writing, then, might open into the possible by creating "a language that does not repeat what the world insists on repeating." Or, as Kaplan so indelibly puts it in the first circle, "Words open the infinite."

NOTES

[1] From the verb "établir," to establish. They "established" themselves, took their places, as workers.

[2] Les gens s'invitent pour montrer leur espace de travail. Jusqu'alors il était interdit d'aller dans un autre atelier que le sien. Pour la première fois, les ouvriers circulent dans leur usine, ce qui paraît extraordinaire: l'usine nous appartient. Surtout, on a le sentiment du temps. Le temps de parler, de se connaître. Je n'avais jamais parlé avec les ouvrières des presses, qui travaillent sur de grosses machines des femmes très fortes, baraquées, qui en rajoutent dans la féminité et le maquillage. Le temps devient le moyen de se rencontrer. Et aussi d'imaginer. ("Spécial mai '68," trans. Jennifer Pap)

[3] Slavoj Zizek. "Afterword: Lenin's Choice." *Revolution at the Gates*. London: Verso, 2002 (263).

[4] Aucun discours ne peut dire l'usine. Il faut des mots suspendus et discordants, ouverts. L'usine, on ne peut pas en finir avec elle par les mots, et les mots qui l'écrivent doivent tenir compte de cela, leur limite. (Kaplan, *L'excès-l'usine*, back cover, trans. Jennifer Pap)

[5] D'autres livres, remarquables, ont décrit le travail de l'usine et à l'usine. Mais

ici et dès les premiers mots, nous comprenons que, si travaillant, nous entrons dans l'usine, nous appartiendrons désormais à l'immensité de l'univers ("*la grande usine univers*"), qu'il n'y aura plus d'autre monde, qu'il n'y en a jamais eu d'autre: fini le temps, abolie la succession, "les choses existent ensemble, simultanées." Il n'y a plus de dehors—vous en sortez? Vous n'en sortez pas.

[6] Le mot pour le dire est encore à inventer. Dire cette activité parcellaire, minuscule, tout le temps identique à elle-même, qui détruit l'individu, le tue dans son génie même, dans son bonheur manuel, dans sa faculté heureuse de rejoindre le dehors….Que l'usine, le lieu décrété sacré du prolétariat, est celui de sa sépulture. (*Les Outils*, 221, trans. Jennifer Pap)

[7] [P]enser avec une oeuvre: avec un objet fini et infini, fabriqué par un homme ou des hommes, et qui, mis en circulation va à la rencontre d'autres hommes, et pourra, ou non, effectivement en rencontrer certains…(*Les Outils*, 9, trans. Jennifer Pap).

[8] For the complete interview, see Kaplan, L., Carr, J., & Pap, J. "There should be battles": Julie Carr and Jennifer Pap interview Leslie Kaplan. Philadelphia, PA: *Jacket2*. http://jacket2.org/interviews/there-should-be-battles

WORKS CITED

Blanchot, Maurice. "*L'Excès-l'Usine* Ou l'Infini Morcelé." *Écrits Politiques*: 1953-1993. Ed. Éric Hoppenot. Paris: Gallimard, 2008.

—"Factory-Excess," or Infinity in Pieces." *Political Writings*: 1953-1993. New York: Fordham University Press, 2010.

Kaplan, Leslie. *L'Excès-l'Usine*. Paris: P.O.L., 1994. First published: 1982, Hachette P.O.L.

—*Les Outils*. Paris: P.O.L., 2003.

—*Mon Amérique commence en Pologne: Depuis maintenant*. Paris: P.O.L., 2009.

—"Spécial Mai 68: Béatrice Vallaeys et Annette Lévy-Willard, Interview avec Leslie Kaplan." *Libération*, 22 May 1998. http://www.liberation.fr/cahier-special/1998/05/22/special-mai-68leslie-kaplan-24-ans-militante-maoiste-ujc-ml-etablie-a-l-usine-brandt-de-lyon-depuis-_235834

—"Writing moves the sky," http://lesliekaplan.net/traductions-translations/article/writing-moves-the-sky

ACKNOWLEDGMENTS

Thank you to the editors of the following journals for publishing some of these translations: *Tripwire*, *Golden Handcuffs*, *Tupelo Quarterly*, and *Asymptote*. Thank you to Commune Editions for supporting this work, first in an earlier chapbook, and now in the full volume. Thank you to Pablo's Café in Denver. And thank you most of all to Leslie Kaplan for encouraging this translation and working closely with us over email and in Paris in October of 2014.